THE HOMAGE

S. J. Litherland

for Wend,
the amazing and always
wonderful !
with love Jackie
x x x x

First published 2006 by IRON Press
5 Marden Terrace, Cullercoats
Northumberland, NE30 4PD
tel/fax: +44 (0)191 253 1901
ironpress@blueyonder.co.uk
www.ironpress.co.uk

ISBN-13 978-0-955245-01-5
ISBN-10 0-9552450-1-X
Printed by Tyneside Free Press,
Newcastle upon Tyne

'Bad Light' was selected for Five Leaves sports anthology *Not Just a Game*
Cover photograph Tom Shaw / ALLSPORT / Getty Images
Cover design by Brian Grogan
IRON Press books
are distributed by Central Books
and represented by Inpress Limited,
Northumberland House,
11 The Pavement, Pope's Lane,
Ealing, London W5 4NG
Tel: +44 (0)20 8832 7464
Fax: +44 (0)20 8832 7465
www.inpressbooks.co.uk

IRON Press is a member of Independent Northern Publishers

CONTENTS

For Jack Litherland *1912-1968*

Ahhh. Lie back, shut your eyes and listen to the traditional sounds of a build up to another England Test series – leather on willow . . . raindrops pelting down . . . knives being sharpened for Nasser Hussain.

Message posted on BBC website

ENGLAND 2003

NASSER HUSSAIN

Hooded eyes of ancestry
wait like a bird of prey

for the flight of the attack,
where will it come this bullet?

wait like a fighter pilot
for the enemy in clear skies

even the air waits impatiently.

You'll have just this moment
this aperture of eye opening

you parry, you stall, you arch
like a bullfighter to the ball.

In the arena there is just you.
The boundary the tempting sea

where the ball must sink gratefully.

Beautiful as a quill pen
you write your legend with elegance.

Through each delivery
you live that dream and wait

a fox surrounded by hounds
to streak away. Chastened

by cunning, your pen is dry.
The bullfighter waits like a statue

for his cue, the head of the ball
lowers to his strike as he kneels

to the sacrifice of himself
to the crowd and his sport.

The bat writes his name with a flourish,
the ball will give you no peace

already it has risen for another coming.

August 26
(116 at Trent Bridge)

ALL NIGHT THE BECK'S ACCOMPANIMENT

All night the beck's accompaniment
to dreams of Nasser's fight back

his salmon leap to the source, instinct
over the thrashing downflow

he will batter his way to the core
his passion's pulse, his first love of cricket.

The salmon does not appraise the flood
he leaps skyward, compelled.

Nasser turns on his oppressors,
shakes his bat, their wily snares blood him

but he's free, out of their carping pages,
beyond their territory, into the uplands.

September 27

BANGLADESH 2003

HUSSAIN AT CHITTAGONG

Butcher, Hussain and Thorpe, battle scarred warriors,
the pack is waiting for them to fall.

They are wily as Odysseus, they have survived.
Each team needs three such veterans,

the young bloods have yet to be tested,
the seasoned are at their prime.

The old warriors keep playing not to be ousted.

Hussain was on battle watch in Chittagong.
He groaned in the heat, the sweat a mask

under his helmet. He was guarding the gate
where the enemy would pour.

All day in the field with one lieutenant
then another. The blood flow stemmed.

No praise for this working, for the toiling,
for occupation of the crease

and the slow ticking of hours,
the runs coming sparse from the grass.

The warrior plays tortoise, content to graft.

The second innings calls him early.

He's too quick for his captain
who fell to the trap

of mistaking one intention for another.

Hussain, the old warhorse, is running from a duck
and the sound of dismay

the non-clapping hands,

sees his captain stranded.

Now every stroke is never enough,
fights in a fury, the warrior reborn,

the scribe is writing: *the shafts from his bat*

are brilliant as light from a mirror.

A great knock of nearly a ton
the boundary his witness

one six and fifteen fours.

Nothing can deny him but destiny.

Bot here yow lakked a little, sir, and lewty yow wanted

The Fates have spun he will perform
a triumph without glory.

This truth is delivered in a single ball
sent back to the hand of his hopetaker.

He raced like a hare and out-ran the field
but his name will not be carved in the pavilion.

He watched like a tiger at the cave of his cubs.
He rampaged like a tiger at the circle of his foes.

But when the games were done
the champion is passed over for a prize.

October 31
(Top Scorer: 76, 95)
lewty – loyalty: Judgment of the Green Knight on Gawain

SRI LANKA 2003

SICKNESS IN THE PAVILION

The score untroubled by your shadow
like the demeanour of a wife
counting breadths of years not moments

yet you're here facing a thousand snipers

like the demeanour of a wife
the score stops the heart of your shadow
yet you're here facing a thousand snipers

he is returning to the camp empty

the score fires the heart of your shadow
the game allows him a second chance
he will not return to the camp empty

his stand is the high price of your sickness

the game will offer him other chances—
counting breadths of years not moments
his success the high price of your sickness

always the hero is troubled by his shadow.

December 7
(Substitute Collingwood holds the fort in his second innings at Galle)

THOUGHTS BETWEEN WICKETS

The station simmers. The station in the hills.
What remains is this field and rancour

for the players. Fans share flags and dance.
The Barmy Army congas, the locals bemused.

The Old Trinitians Club House
is what's upheld of empire rule—and me,

child of the old affair between India
and England, Madras born, Essex bred,

and in my bones and blood I could fight
on either side. The playing fields of Kandy

the English left behind, the game of cricket
bestowed like an imperial seal on grass.

Twice I have to prove myself—
to my ancestors squabbling

in my veins. Every time I raise my bat
I serve my honour. Every time in the attack

the ball is out to shame me, the spell under fire,
all I've had to fight in my name.

It has to be done over and over, after every
century, after each hard-stung catch, after every

defended wicket, after Test after Test.
Cricket is like my forebears, part English,

part Colonial. They all want to take on
The Old Country. I'm that irony:

Anglo-Indian child of love over tyranny,
who plays for his country, his England.

December 13
(Overnight 17* Kandy)

Ruled Out In Colombo

There were complaints made: none proven.

You did not whisper
Cheat Cheat
to the crooked arm bowler.

Every delivery
served up as a ripe apple to bite
every ball
poison.

You spiced
the fatal dish with needling
all hands
against you.

Ambushed by the next ball
the finger raises skyward
quick as a switchblade the decision
the finger raises skyward.

Swift as a guillotine on your neck
you stand there headless,

to the pavilion that long journey
bat under your arm
the condemned man walks,

childhood spent at the nets
everything closed down
to this corridor of bat and ball,

Spartan child always tested

the solitary lesson
of finding skill

is a master not a servant.

Ruled out in Colombo.

Disbelief
at the death of your innings

standing still
as a warrior on the field
who has received news
of his wound but not the message,

carry your lifetime
to the pavilion, dismissed

and must return for punishment
            more of the same
your enemies are whispering
            and prospering.

Your shadow moves into your light.
What you guess you will read
is your obituary.

You have fought their slights
but heads lopped off with your bat
have re-grown.

The honour of the warrior
will always take him
to his last battle, to his defeat
to his loss of prowess

but only the book of Fate tells the hour.

February 5
(unluckily given out lbw first and second innings)

THE WEST INDIES 2004

THE MIDDLE ORDER

The old sweats come to stay.
The young openers
are ball dazzled.

Butcher, Hussain and Thorpe,
tough as thorn bushes,
root in cracks,

old timers know survival,
they can do this,
not with the genius of youth

the heat and the spleen,
the young feet that light sparks
this is slow burning,

this is staying alive
in bad conditions
cautiously edging out

on the soil of changes.
Butcher, Hussain and Thorpe,
a middle order of Zen priests

in white martial outfits
and slender bats as staves
only experience holds the line,

staying there the test
of tests, as runs trickle
like sand in an hourglass

turning over and over.

Ball struck, ball bounced,
artillery puffs of dust

dance a tattoo,
they stir malignly, impenetrable,

heated young bloods take their turns.
The old campaigners dig in.

The platform is built out of battered timber.

March 23
(First and Second Test partnerships)

THE FEAR ALWAYS CARRIED

Hussain sniffs at the crease
fear of the animal

in enemy territory
he's up for a duck

pokes for four
and another

then first ball next day
he knows luck is out

the shooters and the beaters about him

his beak face is scarred
with distress

he peers out of his mask helmet
the look of a raced horse, eyes darting,

his Judas ball
a kiss.

March 26
(Second innings Trinidad)

THE LONELY NOUGHT

The old captain is squiring himself.

Like the old bullfighter
who hopes his bulls will be small,
he studies the field.

He might be called.
He prays his compadres
will see out the innings and victory.

He's padded up. *Only 2 to get –*
but the opener is out
and he must pick up his bat

and greet the next ball.
Walking out to the lonely circle
he weighs chances.

He's seasoned, his nerve chaperoned.
The old captain has leapt like a stag
in the field, still supreme. He nurses

his bat for survival, nerve fading
with the light, his pride corralled.
He keeps risks in his pocket,

plugs his ears to the siren call
of *hit it for four.* Let this cup pass.
Campaigners eye each other.

They know the score. Butcher smiles
as he nods it for one and a no ball.
Both not out as the party begins in the stall.

Hussain's lonely nought has a star.

April 7
(Butcher 16* Hussain 0*, end of Third Test, Series win)

THE THREE CAPTAINS AND A PROPHECY

Two are thinking of strategy
          and one of glory.
Two are thinking of the game
          one of his score.

One climbs as an eagle to the sun
is the highest, the greatest.

Two are thinking on the ground
in the heat and the toil
the long trek through the desert
          the other is flying.

The minds of the two
teem with scheming, antlers
of ideas sprout from their heads.

The other is the lonely daemon.

Two are good captains. One is poor.

The new and the old,
Vaughan and Hussain,
are captains in their brain,

team men, men of unity,

out of their number fighters come.
The line drawn in the sand.

The gods befriend the hero
close the eyes of the umpire with mist,
          snick of ball on bat
lost in the baying of the crowd.

The hero fills his eagle wings. His team
fall away like foothills. From his height
the mountain looms and gods tempt his hubris.

This way is the path to personal greatness,
the highest achievement in cricket.
Only a captain who wants to win would refuse it.

This way to your glory in cricket forever,
Your name will be sung in calypsos.
Only a captain who wants to win would refuse it.

That way you will live forever lower,
your name never etched at this highest level.
But a captain who wants to win would choose it.

The hero succumbed to their favours
and flashed his blade in the empty air,
in his mind he was vanquishing numbers.

He took the cup of fame and drank deeply,
Lara satisfied his thirst at last.

The gods deserted the two good captains.

The new captain fell
to mist in the eyes of the umpire
                                    and shouts
of hope appealing.

The old captain fell too on the sword of exhaustion.
The old guard was crumbling.

Gods watched young warriors replace them,
curbing their instincts to master the field,

curbing their youth and love of great battle,
curbing their spirits to chase every encounter,

to fill themselves with booty on a lost cause.

They remembered their captains in the pavilion,
they remembered old sweats in their defiance,

and tempered their swords into shields,
and Lara fumbled as Fate slipped from his fingers.

Destined to win for himself but not for his team.

From the moment of his glory he cast down
their chances, handed his team to darkness,
to bottom of the league in Hades gloom

while the two wily captains, the old and new,
soar to bright branches with the few.

April 13
(Prophecy of a Drawn Game in the Fourth Test,
after Lara's World Record 400 runs delayed
his declaration and reduced time for victory)

ENGLAND 2004

BAD LIGHT

The ruffled flags, deep bank of trees under gloom,

cold eddies of air, the swaddled wicket,
no-one sitting on the terraces,

this the coal face of a dank dark day,
the Riverside windy bowl unstirred

by strokes, empty of attention. Members sit
at white clothed tables hoping. Nasser's opening.

Held onto like a talisman.

This the place of slow appreciation
and the contemplation of the circle.

Only those who keep the game are here,
no TV, no crowds, no glamour,

the enactment of a rite passed on
by rules, history and pleasure.

The verse patterns that weave
the great battles and small,

the slow heroic sweep of epic time,
each delivery a line in stanzaic overs,

runners crossing like harpists' hands,
each delivery point and counter point,

question and reply like an ancient choir.

Batsmen flamboyant as chiefs
who fought battles in couplets of poetry.

The strung out fielders set as a trap,
as one by one the bowlers

connive to lure these heroes
to the pavilion. It's what keeps us waiting,

patience learnt like the ancient art of listening.

May 8
(Bad light stops play: Durham v Essex)

THE HOMAGE

The dawn mist persisting and persisting,
waiting for the heavy veil to lift for cricket
to commence, for me to wait like a sentry

as Nasser passes and chats to an Essex man
and catches my eye, a cat to a king staring,
and when he comes off, the glance again

knitting up eyes, this is as close as it gets
to the muse, this quiet warm-up off-guard
moment, time for him to autograph

a small boy's notebook. "He doesn't always"
the Essex man says. He strides past later,
helmet on, padded up, transformed

to public warrior. This is his work today,
opening the batting. The five slips say
it is a cold damp dark morning. Nothing

dramatic as he protects his wicket
and then a sudden snap of aggression,
a stance cracked open like a dancer's

belligerence, electric shock of attitude,
the stance of the Indian death goddess
Kali, a warning struck of her temper

in a long innings for 70, in sixes
and boundaries. The class in the gesturing
on this small stage closed down by weather.

In the damp air the slips hover like gnats,
everyone is caught today in their netting.
Out of myself I finally pay this homage,

out of a childhood of attrition
and punishment and the mutiny
of hatred, out of a girl's defiance

of the man with purple lips who hit her,
I finally own what I owe to my father,
his love of cricket passed on with the tying

of rags into a ball and a propped up wicket.
Homage to something I couldn't consider
sitting in closed rooms watching The Test,

the legends Bradman, Hutton, Denis Compton,
the calypsos and the reverence to Sobers,
and to my county, Warwickshire, where

wartime back streets were my pitches.
Nothing to be admitted, much as Nasser's
beating back of a ball constantly thrown

like criticism no matter what you do
or reply. My childhood rite of passage
to this arena of parsimonious attendance

on a dank day as the whites bravely flutter
on dismal grass and my muse accelerates
his impatience with spin bowling

and he's halfway down the pitch to meet
his assailant as though to say *this*
is my autograph to the small boys watching,

I've come in homage although delayed,
what thou lovest well remains, the poet says,
and I'm here all day with the cricket.

May 10
the poet: Ezra Pound: Pisan Cantos

THE KNIVES

He will drag himself across a thousand knives
for the prize of a hundred caps.

    The envious one spoke*: Drop him* –

timely, caught him unawares after praise.
I have served my country well. Hussain
in mid play falters. The knife from this foe,

from that quarter, from his own camp,
as he prepares once more for battle.
He was out in the field, feinting strokes,

his reflex his great fortune, fast
as a young man's, sharp as a sabre.
Wounded he must recover, wounded

he falls at the practice, other knives
will follow. They killed
his captaincy, flawed him fatally.

The old warrior must face them again.
Five more Tests to his prize, the great accolade
for service, no more than that

and none greater.

May 14

AUBADE

This dawn is refusing to come to light, this beautiful
untouched May morning with dove call and bird chatter
and scent of jasmine. Anxiety about Nasser pervades

and the poetry of the dawn sits outside my window.
These lines are sent in sympathy from one admirer
of his art, his solitary figure against detractors

and one particular bully who has called for his bat
to be surrendered. I wonder if this is 'cricket' or some
gladiatorial contest or unlovely ancient trait,

this tendency for arenas of taunting where a creature
can be baited, preferably one like you who will fight.
And here I am again in this circle of childhood

without answers to what I learnt from my father.
Sunlight announces on the roofs the dawn
is over and time for anxiety foreclosing, the birds

quiet except for a single cooing dove, the lonely
breath of early traffic and the wind rush of a train
over the viaduct. Illumination is what we have

after anger against injustice, the spirit defines us.
Nasser, you're an artist in your temperament
and give your soul to the game which is an elegant

arrangement of a pair fighting against the many,
and when the ball comes to you it is every jibe
you've encountered. Cricket a pattern of rules,

life rewritten as fair play where each takes a turn
in being tested, each side the symmetry of attack
and defence. It is the sport's gift to have umpires

oversee manners and comportment. This day
a perfect May morning, the sky that English blue
that has a touch of mauve against the fresh green trees

flawless until an early plane hems its way across,
so high its wake of sound is no louder than a bee.
The tassels of wisteria gently lengthen in the sun

their Chinoiserie opening with the hawthorn flowers.
On such a day Morris Men and cricket teams set forth
in their whites, the colour has the significance

of equality. The revolution keeps its tryst
in this rustic game, Leveller code, from each according
to his ability the team is made and a leader respected.

In this disenfranchised country, deregulated
and unkempt, the trooping of cricket teams onto mown
greens is the solace renewed of our lost history

where *Jerusalem* was a vision of a fair society
to be built by simple villagers taking back their land,
where the Diggers took their stand on the commons,

games handed down on the model of their sympathies.
We are illuminated by our sport keeping faith in their
practices. In this spirit, Nasser, your bat is not for burning.

May 15

ROME

The auditorium is set
for a morning of torture

The gladiatorial games
have begun

His enemies have won
the uneven contest over

He must fight to end his life
gracefully

The great summit out of reach

Their viciousness
will be remembered

Their lies, their campaigns
to bring him down

Nasser they chose you
to suffer

always you answered
your tormentors

I salute you

May 22
(Before start of play, day 2
First New Zealand Test, Lords)

His Name Will Be Carved In The Pavilion

Bounce higher golden ball
Bounce higher
and he will catch it
with his golden bat.

This is how it was on the morning of this story
how it began in May sunshine, the last day
of five days of two countries in contention,

how the battle swung between England and New Zealand.
How there were many moments in a long game
like sparkling sun on water, this was a great Test

of three centuries and high scores, batsmen
striking the ball like the tongues of lizards,
Nasser taking four wickets with the brilliance

of his fielding, of two high leaping catches
as if he could fly like a dryad, and when he aimed
the ball for stumping the bails jumped for joy.

The reserve captain and his next-in-line fell early.
The ground hushed as England stumbled drawing
in the net of fielders to tighten at her throat.

The New Zealanders were buoyant
as Nasser strode in buckled up for battle.
His experience and the young lieutenant held the field.

The young contender who was another shadow
for his place, another young one to depose the king.
Nasser was foxy as his foil and his tether, to let

the young one climb higher as he guarded the gate.
Nasser the watchman who does his duty at the bridge
holding the pass while the enemy was striving and tiring.

In the quiet of the day under May sunshine,
in the quiet of the hour they eased England
out of her trouble, only two holes in her seacraft

as she was steadied onto her journey, that sea torn
journey rocked by fire from enemy guns.
Orders from the reserve captain came. Steady enough,

but you must move faster and make runs.
Then came the calamitous moment.
The two stranded in the middle of the wicket

at Nasser's call, as if they had come to the wrong
room and were trying to find the exit.
The gods whispered in Nasser's ear. *Run to your wicket*

and safety. Let the young man fall.
But youth had acquitted itself with honour.
Nasser turned to stumping and ignominy,

into the arms of his enemies, back to be ousted.
The young lieutenant saw his intention
and raced ahead to overtake his maestro,

like young heroes of old who press into the fray
when they see their lord in danger.
To the death of his dream ran the contender,

his name carved twice in the pavilion,
Andrew Strauss in the making of a legend.
Dismay was the bitter sweat of the one

who was spared, bitter sweat salty on nervous lips
and the incoming Thorpe saw his distress
and touched his arm with comfort that said *let's do it.*

Then two of England's henchmen, Thorpe and Hussain,
set about their duty as New Zealanders were whooping.
All the skill those New Zealanders could offer, all the patience

with the deceiving ball, like a kiss that must be rejected.
The two old warriors stood on trial together.
They knitted the pattern of this saga,

knitting the story as they hurried between wickets
slowly raising the total out of sights of the guns.
They attacked with high bats after patience was done,

Nasser advancing to greet the wayward ball
like a bridegroom to the feast, like a man who
has listened to every argument and has one answer.

The day in the field was nearly over and he was young
with the grimness of satisfaction, the heavy armour
of defence fell off his shoulders, his bat lighter

than the foe's weary arms as sunlight lengthened.
The pair weighed up the cozening of their wickets
and path to personal glory laid with traps.

Just 27 runs to make and keep their wickets firm.
Hussain had been climbing to high numbers
and Thorpe towards the middle range. Their quick glances

told them, quick as decisions of warriors testing
their agility with heavy armour to run the distance.
Let us count down as they reached the final overs,

those six-stringed lutes on which they play the song
of this story. Only 13 runs to chase after Thorpe
reached his 50 and saluted his bat to the pavilion

and the standing cheering chorus of approval.
Hussain has reached his 90s but the clock
is ticking, the clock of ticking singles as they share

between wickets. He stands at 94 with 9 runs
at their disposal before the end of the match,
victory and applause, and the hesitation of this story

to reach higher ground. There were singles not taken
as the ball sulked to grant Nasser his moment
of greatness. The cup came to him as he took strike:

would he drink or pass over? He could safely single
England to victory. He could take the lesser glory.
The Fates watched as three balls were stifled.

He took the cup and girded himself. He took the cup.
The ball flew from his bat, like a hawk soaring
out of his hand to the prey of the boundary.

He stood at 98 and breathed deeply. He breathed
the deep rarefied air of a legendary moment
and met it with his high bat. The ball streaked

away, like a hare leaping through fending hands
to the safety of the border, where the crowd
had been waiting to explode into a great storm

roar as when lightning strikes the earth,
taking him past the century for his name
to be carved in the pavilion at Lords.

The casting away of his doubts into the crowd's
clapping hands where they landed safely,
the hands of 20,000 shouting him yes

and Hussain raises his bat to the heavens
and the four corners of the ground. His face
illuminated by candle flames of his eyes.

Then the last ball came singing down
for another great strike, it sang like a cantata
to the boundary. It sang of victory

and the legend to be told of three golden strokes.
In the middle the two warriors embraced.
Their work was over and so is mine in this story.

May 25
(England beat New Zealand at Lords by 7 wickets)

THE RETIREMENT OF NASSER HUSSAIN

Words flew around the country to save you,
you weren't listening. If I could I would have risen

100 feet above ground and taken the cloud
to hide you in until the media birds scattered,

those pecking your eyes. On another stage
the whispering started into flocks of gulls squabbling

for a place on the rocks. You were the fire warrior:
the kicked down flame that will leap back again,

the ember of anger, the stubborn lozenge of glow
in ashes that would spit, the ever hungry passion

but you changed your shape into water and
put ambition out. You brought me beautiful

gifts, an ornate chiselled bracelet of your
century at Lords with matching inlaid necklace

of the game you won. My muse was not staying.
The key had melted in the firebomb he threw.

May 27

DRAMATIS PERSONAE

Nasser Hussain	*Captain of England 1999-2003*
Mark Butcher, Graham Thorpe	*England middle order batsmen*
Michael Vaughan	*Captain of England*
Andrew Strauss	*Debutant batsman May 2004*
Reserve captain	*Marcus Trescothick May 2004*
The shadow	*Paul Collingwood, substitute for Hussain*
Crooked arm bowler	*Muttiah Muralitharan, ace Sri Lanka spin bowler*
Brian Lara	*Captain of West Indies 2004*

CRICKETING TERMS IN THE POEMS

Boundary: roughly circular edge of cricket field; 4 runs awarded to batsman by ball hit to the boundary: ball clearing the boundary without a bounce is awarded 6 runs. (Both highly regarded).

Century, a ton: 100 runs (highly prized), hence the 'nervous nineties' as batsmen near the mark. A Test Century merits the batsman's name added to the roll of honour in the Pavilion.

Fifty: 50 runs, a sturdy achievement requiring the batsman to raise his bat to the crowd.

Pavilion: covered seating area for Cricket Club Members, players' balcony, changing rooms, Members' bar and lounge.

Over: set of six deliveries by bowler.

Delivery: run up and bowling of ball to batsman.

Barmy Army: self-styled English fans, rowdy but good-tempered.

Nets: netted wickets for practice.

Wicket/pitch: specially prepared oblong of turf in centre of field where two batsmen play.

Wicket: three wooden sticks topped by two wooden bails batsmen defend. (Stumps, same thing)

Wicket, loss of: when batsman is out.

Duck: out for nought (especially dreaded). Pair of ducks, nought in consecutive innings (even worse). The allusion is to the shape of the duck's egg = nought.

The score/scorers not troubled: no runs added

*: star against score or batsman's name: not out.

Slips: fielders placed behind batsman to catch ball coming off the edge of the bat. Nine slips is the record. A slip cordon like this used to seriously intimidate lower order batsman facing a fast bowler.

Openers: two batsmen at 1, 2, who open the innings.

Innings: each team has two innings to bat and score runs in a Test match.

Test: five day match between nations in International League (especially gruelling hence name).

Middle order: batsmen, usually at 3, 4, 5, all-rounders at 6, 7, tail: bowlers batting, usually 8, 9, 10, 11.
Platform: substantial enough number of runs for the team to defend. Varies according to pitch.
Occupation of the crease: batting defensively (often after several wickets lost called a collapse).
Old, veteran, etc: any experienced long serving player Thirty Something.
unlucky: wrongly given out by umpire.
finger raised: gesture by umpire giving batsman out.

NOTES

Cricket lore has it that the sport began in an English open field in early mediaeval times, probably on turf grazed by sheep, probably by shepherd boys playing against the wicket gate of a sheep pen.
This small wooden gate consisted of two uprights and a crossbar on top, called a bail, which fitted into slots. A ball would be fashioned of wool tied in twine and a crook used as a bat. Early versions of the cricket bat were curved. Early wickets were two stumps and a bail. (The modern game of three stumps and two bails dates from 1786.)
To aid sighting the ball against white attire, it is likely it was dyed in red ochre, traditionally used for marking sheep. To this day cricket balls are red. The length of a cricket pitch has never altered from 22 yards – the measurement of the agricultural chain.
The crease (now a line of whitewash) where batsmen stand was once a mark cut into turf.
The cricket ground is still called a field with fielders.
Cricce/crice – Anglo-Saxon for stick. Stumps is derived from Old Norse stumpr.

S. J. Litherland

learnt to love cricket as a child in her home county of
Warwickshire. Since 1965 she has lived in Durham and is a
member of Durham County Cricket Club. *The Homage* is her
fifth collection of poetry. Previous collections: *The Work of the Wind*
(Flambard 2006), *The Apple Exchange* (Flambard 1999), *Flowers of Fever*
(IRON 1992) and *The Long Interval* (Bloodaxe 1986).

Winner of two Northern Writers' Awards, her work has appeared in
various anthologies, notably the Bloodaxe *New Women Poets,*
The Forward Book of Poetry 2001, North by North-East (IRON 2006)
and the Russian *Modern Poets of Northern England.* She has edited many
books including *The Poetry of Perestroika* (IRON, with Peter Mortimer)
and is a founding member of Vane Women writers' collective and press.
A former journalist she now teaches Creative Writing.
She has four grandsons.

Reviews for S. J. Litherland's previous poetry collection

THE WORK OF THE WIND

'*The Work of the Wind* is a wild storm of words, extreme emotions and wonderful poems . . . But it is also a brave attempt to make meaning out of memory, an assertion that, through poetry, "the idea of order is presiding over the nature of fragments."'
Andy Croft, The Morning Star

'*The Work of the Wind* is a great book, reminiscent in some ways of MacNeice's Autumn Journal in its charting of time with references to events both personal and universal. She has harnessed the wind, rescued the tumbling memories from potential chaos, and allowed it to move her forward in a burst of passionate creative energy.'
Jo Colley, Kenaz

'. . . a deeply impressive demonstration of how life's pains can be turned to artistic gain . . . Very often the failures in human relationships go to the making of poems angry, self-pitying, bereft. In *The Work of the Wind* we have an exploration of the territory carried out in an unflinching, forgiving and resolved spirit. Poetically achieved, the work here offers an important model of contemporary absolution.'
Michael Standen, Other Poetry

'An excellent new collection – *The Work of the Wind* – from S. J. Litherland sits on top of my reading pile.'
Kitty Fitzgerald, Scotland on Sunday

'. . . a tour de force, a mesmerizing display of technique and range, a tremendous epitaph to a poet (Barry MacSweeney) and a love story just in case you weren't hooked already.'
Anna Filacksis, Bee website

'So, to the highpoint of the night, an appearance from top northern poet Jackie Litherland supported by the Hydrogen Jukebox cabaret team performing from Jackie's wonderful new book, *The Work of the Wind*.'
Bob Nichols, Middlesbrough Evening Gazette

Published by Flambard Press at £8.50.